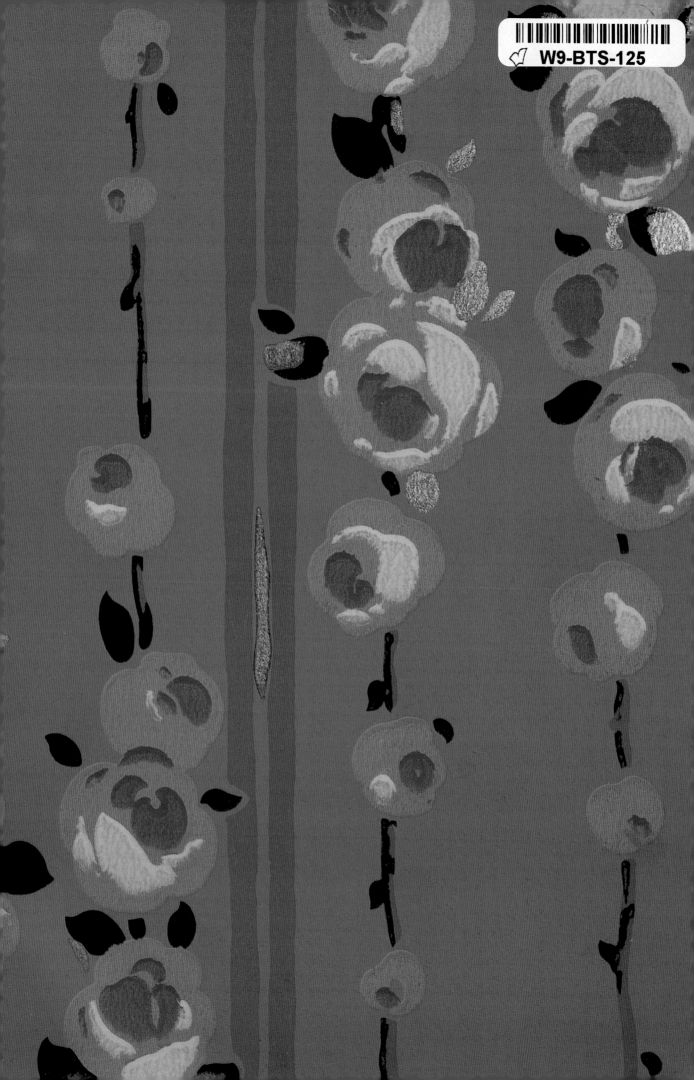

A House Blessing

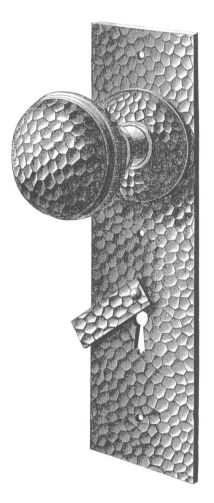

A
House

Blessing

BY WELLERAN POLTARNEES
BLUE LANTERN BOOKS · MCMXCVI

ISBN 1-883211-04-2

Blue Lantern Books
PO Box 4399, Seattle, Washington, 98104

I bless this house
and all those who dwell within it, and wish
for them a full portion of
life's beauty.

1

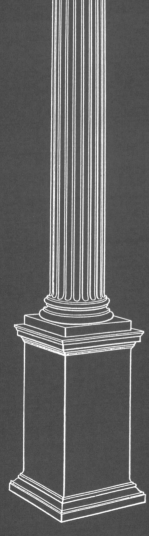

May the strength of its walls make you safe, keeping peace within and trouble without;

3

but through its open
windows and doors let
nature come.

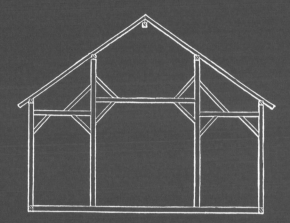

All who live and visit here shall be friends.
Kindliness and harmony shall be
the watchwords.

Let the mealtimes be far more than
the fulfillment of a necessity.
In this home food shall be prepared
with grace, and eaten with
gratitude.

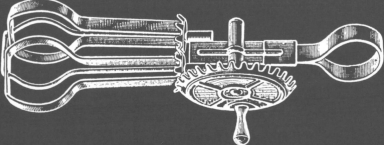

May this be a place where the laughter of babies is heard,

11

and the gravity of
children is answered
with loving respect.

13

Make this house warm in the
winter, and by the fires of an
open hearth let comradeship
and imagination flower.

When the sun is ablaze,
here shall coolness and
shade hold sway.

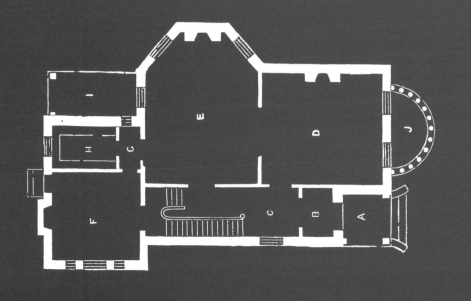

Let this be the place of peace, offering
refuge from chaos and
doubt, and manifesting
in its orderliness, a
model for the larger world.

I wish for all of you the blessings of the night, which blanket us with calm, and through its burning stars and liquid moonlight allows our hearts to flower.

21

May beauty reign
here, and lovely
objects renew us by
their silence and
perfection.

I wish for you, in this
sheltered place, the
freedom, calm and
leisure to play and
explore.

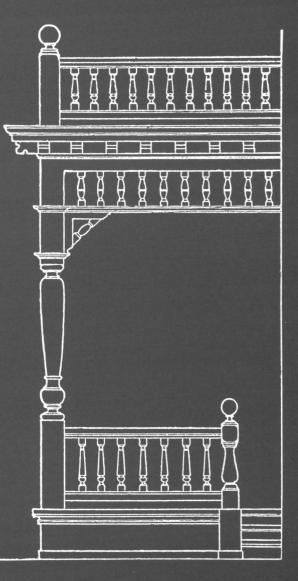

May all celebrations be, in this house, feasts
of creativity and companionship.

Bless this house.
May angels guard its corners, and may
gifts fall upon it as snow falls upon a field.
Let those within it share numberless
passages of the sun and moon,
and happiness fill them to overflowing.

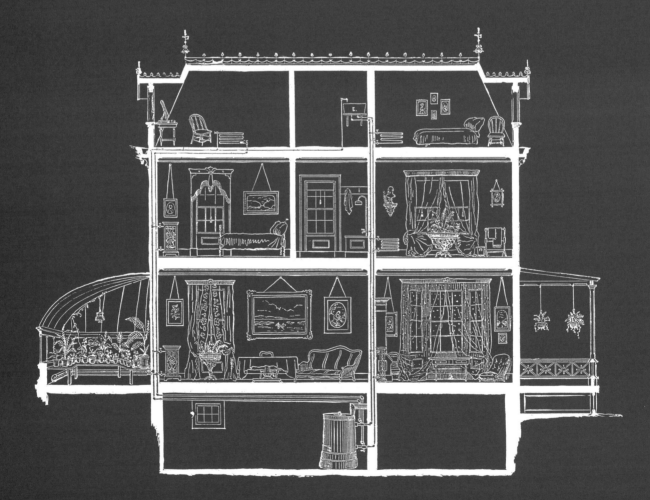

Picture Credits

Front cover	Kent, Rockwell. Advertising pamphlet. 1939
Frontispiece	Parrish, Maxfield. "Ottaqueeche River." 1947
Title Page	Anonymous. Advertising pamphlet. 1923
Copyright page	Kent, Rockwell. Advertising pamphlet. 1939
Endpapers	French wallpaper. circa 1925
1	E.W. Advertising pamphlet. n.d.
2	Vogeler, Heinrich. "Matinée de Mai." 1907
3	Moll, Carl. "Interieur." 1903
4	Larsson, Carl. "The Flower Window." circa 1895
5	Kent, Rockwell. Advertising pamphlet. 1939
6	de Jonghe, Gustave. "Intimité." n.d.
7	Anonymous. Magazine advertisement. 1945
8	Digs, W. Magazine advertisement. 1925.
9	Paxton, William McGregor. "The Kitchen Maid." 1907
10	Hitchcock, Lucius W. Magazine advertisement. 1924
11	Saida. Magazine advertisement. 1923
12	Le Mair, H. Willebeek. from *Little People.* 1915
13	Winter, Alice Beach. Magazine illustration. circa 1910
14	Murray, J.K. Magazine cover. 1931
15	E.O. Magazine illustration. 1922
16	Hammershoi, Vilhelm. "Dust Motes Dancing in The Sunlight." 1900
17	Halpert, Samuel. "Women Reading in an Interior." 1925
18	Larsson, Carl. "Catch-up Homework in Summertime." 1902
19	Mourgne, P. Magazine cover. 1927
20	Anonymous. Magazine advertisement. 1921
21	Spiegel, Ferdinand. "Abend am Tegernsee." n.d.
22	Coleman, Charles Caryl. "Studio Window, Isle of Capri." 1897
23	De Camp, Joseph. "The Blue Cup." 1909
24	Taylor, Leonard Campbell. "Chess." 1908
25	Gow, M.L. "Fairy Tales." 1880
26	Bains, Ethel F.B. Magazine advertisement. 1917
27	Brate, Fanny. Untitled. 1902
29	Hopper, Edward. "Room in Brooklyn"(detail). 1932
Back cover	Kent, Rockwell. "Lilacs." circa 1968

This book was typeset in Bernhard Modern.

Book & cover design by Sacheverell Darling at Blue Lantern Studio.

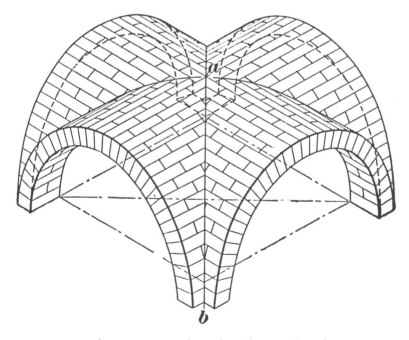

Printed in Hong Kong through P. Chan & Edward, Inc.